Carnival Readers

I Hop

Written by
S. Rance

© Copyright text S. Rance 1994
© Copyright illustrations Macmillan Education Ltd 1994

All rights reserved. No reproduction, copy or transmission of
this publication may be made without written permission.

No paragraph of this publication may be reproduced, copied or
transmitted save with written permission or in accordance with
the provisions of the Copyright, Designs and Patents Act 1988,
or under the terms of any licence permitting limited copying issued
by the Copyright Licensing Agency, 90 Tottenham Court Road,
London W1P 9HE.

Any person who does any unauthorised act in relation to this
publication may be liable to criminal prosecution and civil
claims for damages.

First published 1994
Reprinted 1995

Published by MACMILLAN EDUCATION LTD
London and Basingstoke
*Associated companies and representatives in Accra, Banjul,
Cairo, Dar es Salaam, Delhi, Freetown, Gaborone, Harare,
Hong Kong, Johannesburg, Kampala, Lagos, Lahore, Lusaka,
Mexico City, Nairobi, São Paulo, Tokyo*

ISBN 0-333-61804-1

Printed in Hong Kong

A catalogue record for this book is available from the
British Library.

Illustrations by *Frances Cary*

I hop
I hop
I do not stop.

I hop
over the house
of the little grey mouse.

We hop
We hop
We do not stop.

I hop
over the cat
in the big red hat.

We hop
We hop
We do not stop.

I hop
over the dog
and the big green frog.

We hop
We hop
We do not stop.

I hop
on the nose
of the elephant named Rose.

We hop
We hop
We do not stop.

I hop
on the tail
of a lion named Dale.

We hop
We hop
We do not stop.

I hop
under a giraffe
and make it laugh.

We hop
We hop
We do not stop.

I hop
into a plane
and out again.

We hop
We hop
We do not stop.

I hop
over a bee
in a little green tree.

We hop
We hop
We do not stop.

I hop
round and round
then up and down.

Stop! Stop!
We are tired and hot!

So now I stop.

Words to learn for this book

mouse   cat   frog
elephant   lion   giraffe
laugh   plane

Reading comprehension questions

1. Does the boy hop on the elephant's tail?
2. Does the boy hop over the giraffe?
3. Does the boy hop round the plane?
4. What colour is the mouse?
5. What colour is the cat's hat?